SASHIKO TABLE LINENS

The simplicity of traditional Japanese sashiko embroidery is given a new life with contrasting colours.
By Jemima Schlee

YOU WILL NEED

- 4" diameter cardboard circle
- 3/4 yd of four different colors of 43"/44" wide linen (each 3/4 yd will make one place mat, one napkin and one napkin holder)
- 3/4 yd of 43"/44" wide sew-in quilting fleece (will make all 4 place mats)
- 7/8" diameter button cover kit
- 1/8" diameter elastic cord
- Air-soluble fabric pen
- Ruler
- Embroidery needle
- Embroidery floss (to contrast with your linens – two skeins of each color)
- Sewing needle
- Scissors
- Pins
- Sewing thread to match your linen colors
- Sewing machine and an iron

Always match the fabric right sides and raw edges when sewing.

FOR EACH PLACE MAT

1 Cut two pieces of linen 13" x 17". Cut a piece of quilting fleece 12" x 16". Center the fleece on one piece of linen. Stitch around the fleece edges, stitching close to each edge (*image 1*).

2 Place this piece of linen on top of the other linen piece. Pin all around. Leaving a 5" opening on one short edge for turning, stitch the linen layers together about 1/8" from the fleece edge. Backstitch at the beginning and end of the seam for strength.

3 Trim the corners and turn right side out. Press the raw edges to the inside. Slipstitch the opening closed (*image 2*).

TIP

Using a thimble helps to draw your embroidery floss through your linen, particularly when working through more than two layers at the edges.

PHOTOS: EMMA NOREN; STEP PHOTOS: JEMIMA SCHLEE

INTERLOCKING CIRCLE DESIGN

4 Lay the place mat out as it would be on a table. Use the air-soluble pen and a ruler to draw a horizontal and a vertical line, dissecting your mat into four equal parts. Center the cardboard circle on the center intersection and draw around it with the pen. Draw another circle above the first one, centered on the vertical line; draw another below the first circle. Their curved edges should just touch each other. Threading your embroidery needle with all six strands of a contrasting color floss, work Running Stitches along the drawn lines, stitching through all three layers of the mat. Continue drawing around the template and stitching (*image 3*), following the interlocking circle design (*page 5*), until the whole mat is covered with stitched circles.

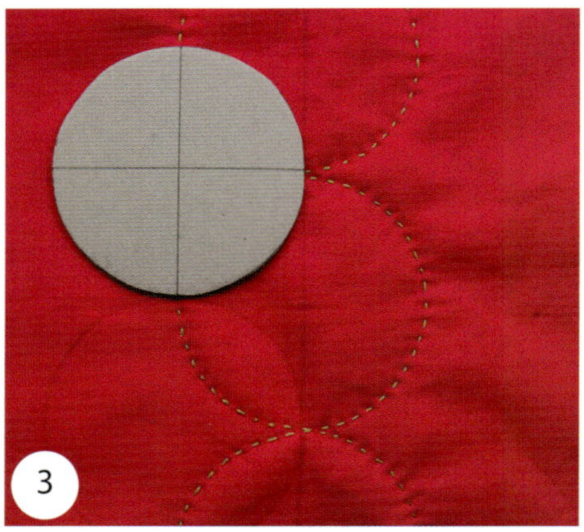

3

CHECKED DESIGN

5 Lay the place mat out as it would be on a table. Use the air-soluble pen and a ruler to draw a horizontal and a vertical line, dissecting your mat into four equal parts. Threading your embroidery needle with all six strands of a contrasting color floss, work Running Stitches along the drawn lines, stitching through all three layers of the mat. Using a ruler, draw lines 3/8" on either side of the lines and work Running Stitches along the lines. Leaving 1 1/2" gaps, draw and stitch three lines (3/8" apart) across the rest of your mat, horizontally and vertically, following the checked design (*page 5*).

FOR EACH NAPKIN

6 Cut an 18" x 18" square from linen. Press 1/2" fold to the wrong side on all four edges. Press 1/2" to the wrong side again.

7 Threading the embroidery needle with all six strands of a contrasting color floss, work Running Stitches through all layers to both decorate the border and anchor the hem (*image 4*); press.

4

FOR EACH NAPKIN HOLDER

8 Cut a piece of linen 2 3/4" x 7 1/2" Matching the long edges, fold in half and press. Slip a 3" loop of elastic cord in one of the short ends (*image 5*). Using a 1/4" seam allowance, stitch along the long edge and the short edge, catching the cord in the stitchng. Stitch back and forth over the cord ends several times for strength.

5

9 Turn the holder right side out through the open short end. Fold the raw edges in 1/4" and press.

10 Threading the embroidery needle with all six strands of a contrasting color floss, work Running Stitches around all four edges to secure the open end and decorate the border; press.

11 Follow the manufacturer's instructions to cut a piece of linen for the covered button. Using all six strands of floss, work Running Stitches to create a pattern on the linen. Cover the button. Sew the button on the linen strip at the end opposite the elastic loop (*image 6*).

6

SHASHIKO TABLE LINENS

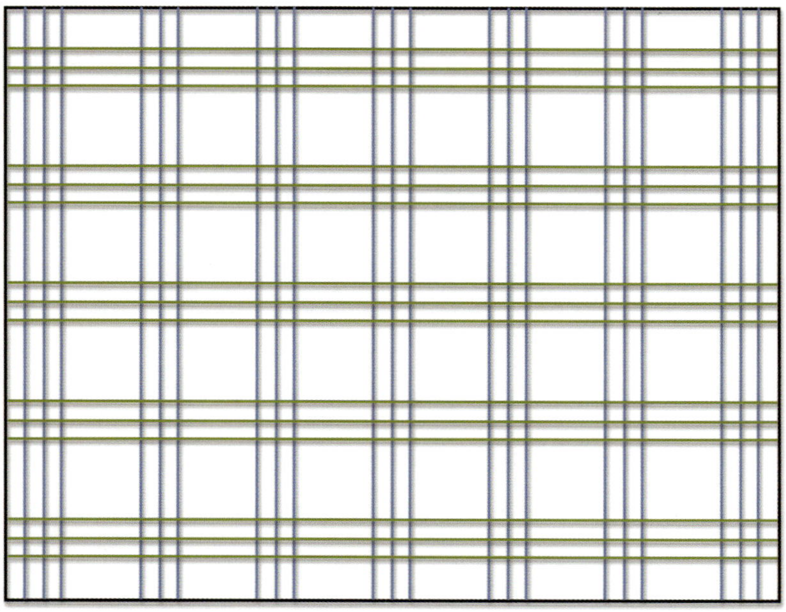

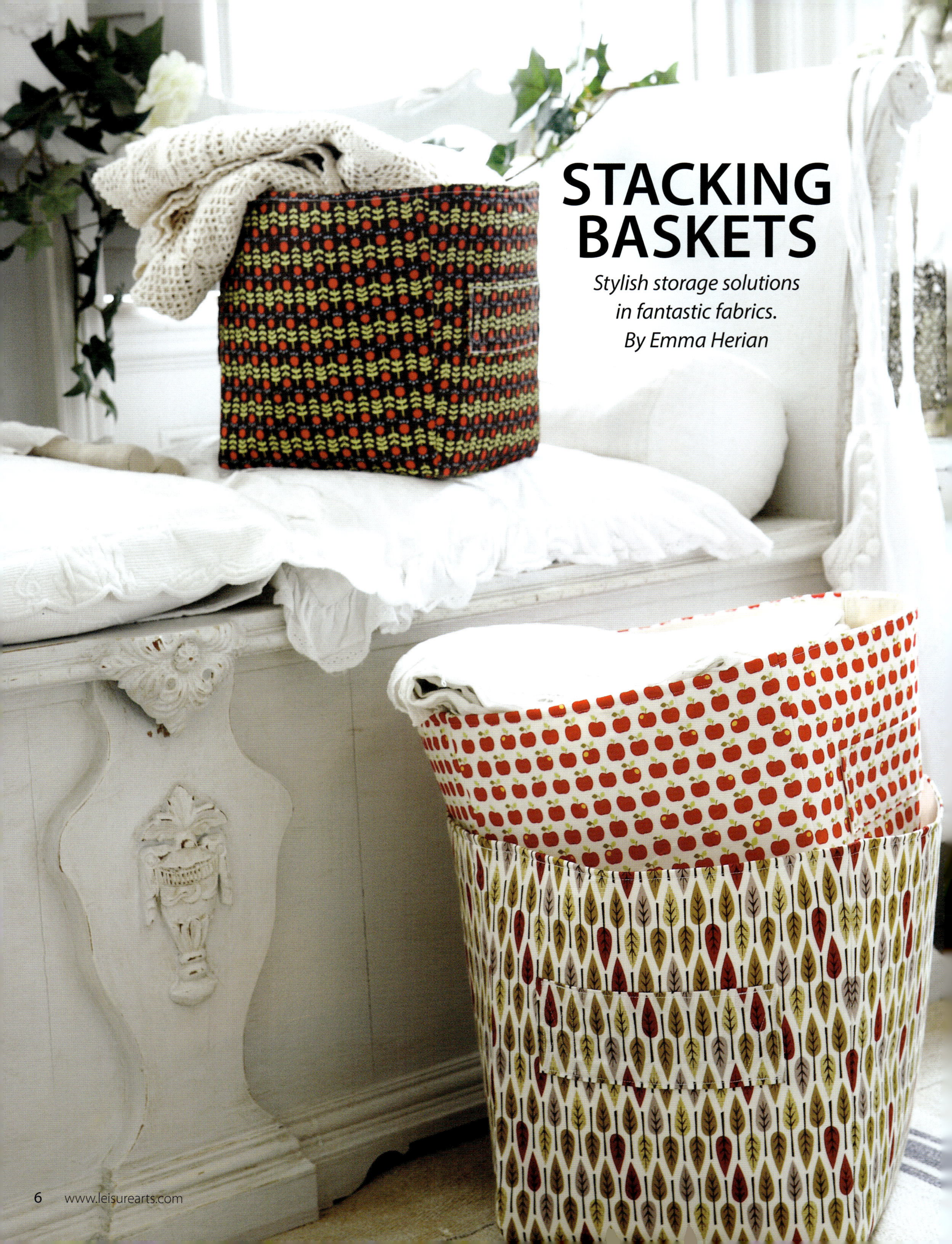

STACKING BASKETS

Stylish storage solutions in fantastic fabrics.

By Emma Herian

YOU WILL NEED

- **Large basket:** 7/8 yd of 43/44" wide patterned fabric
- **Medium basket:** 3/4 yd of 43/44" wide patterned fabric
- **Small basket:** 3/4 yd of 43/44" wide patterned fabric
- 3/4 yd of 58"/60" wide heavy muslin or duck for lining
- 2 yds of 20" wide heavyweight sew-in craft interfacing
- Sewing machine
- Thread
- Pins
- Scissors
- Iron

Always match the fabric right sides and raw edges and use a 1/2" seam allowance when sewing.

1 You will find the pattern pieces on pages 8-9. Photocopy the patterns at 206%. The following process is for the large basket. Use the patterns to cut 4 large side panel pieces of the patterned fabric, muslin and interfacing. Then cut 1 large base piece from the same fabrics. Using the patterned fabric, cut 2 pieces for the handles using the large handle pattern.

TIPS

Make sure your patterns on the fabric are all facing up the right way before cutting.

Snipping the corners will make the edges crisp and help when turning right side out.

2 Matching the wrong sides, fold the handles in half lengthwise. Press on the fold and open up, fold and press a 1/2" border all the way round then fold in half using the original crease (*image 1*). Press again, then topstitch close to the edges.

1

3 Place one patterned fabric side panel on top of the interfacing side panel, right side up. Center the handle, 4" from the top (wider) edge, and pin in place (*image 2*).

2

4 At either end sew the handle to the side panel using a box-cross stitch pattern to reinforce the handle. Repeat the process for the other handle on another side panel (*image 3*).

3

5 To sew the sides to the base, take the patterned fabric base piece and place on top of interfacing base piece. Matching the narrow edges, pin one of the handle side panels to one edge of the base; start sewing 1/2" in from the edge and stop sewing 1/2" before you get to the end (*image 4*). Make sure you backstitch at either end. Snip the corner and press the seam. Repeat process on all sides, making sure the handles are opposite each other.

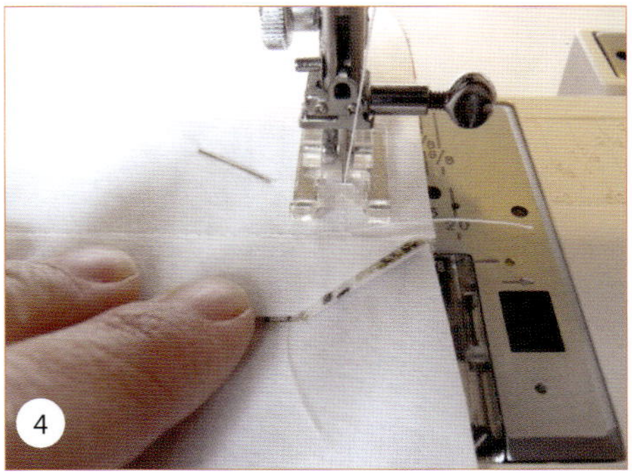
4

MAIN PHOTOGRAPHS: LAUREL GUILFOYLE; STEP PHOTOS: EMMA HERIAN

6 Carefully sew two sides together starting from the base, making sure you start 1/2" in as before and allowing a 1/2" seam allowance; sew all the way to the top, then backstitch. Snip the corners and press. Repeat this method until all sides are sewn and you have a basket shape. Carefully turn the basket right side out.

7 Repeat steps 5 and 6 using the muslin to create the lining. Press all seams and a 3/4" hem to the wrong side along the top of the lining.

8 Fold a 1/2" hem along the top edge of the patterned exterior basket and press. Place the muslin lining inside the patterned basket, wrong sides together, so that the seams all match up; pin in place (*image 5*).

5

9 Stitch close to the lining edge to attach the lining to the exterior basket (*image 6*).

10 Repeat Steps 1-9 to create the medium and small size baskets.

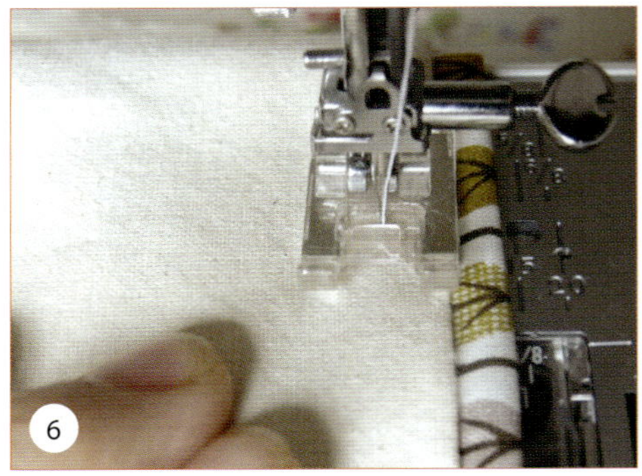

6

STACKING BASKETS

Photocopy the patterns at 206%

Photocopy the patterns at 206%

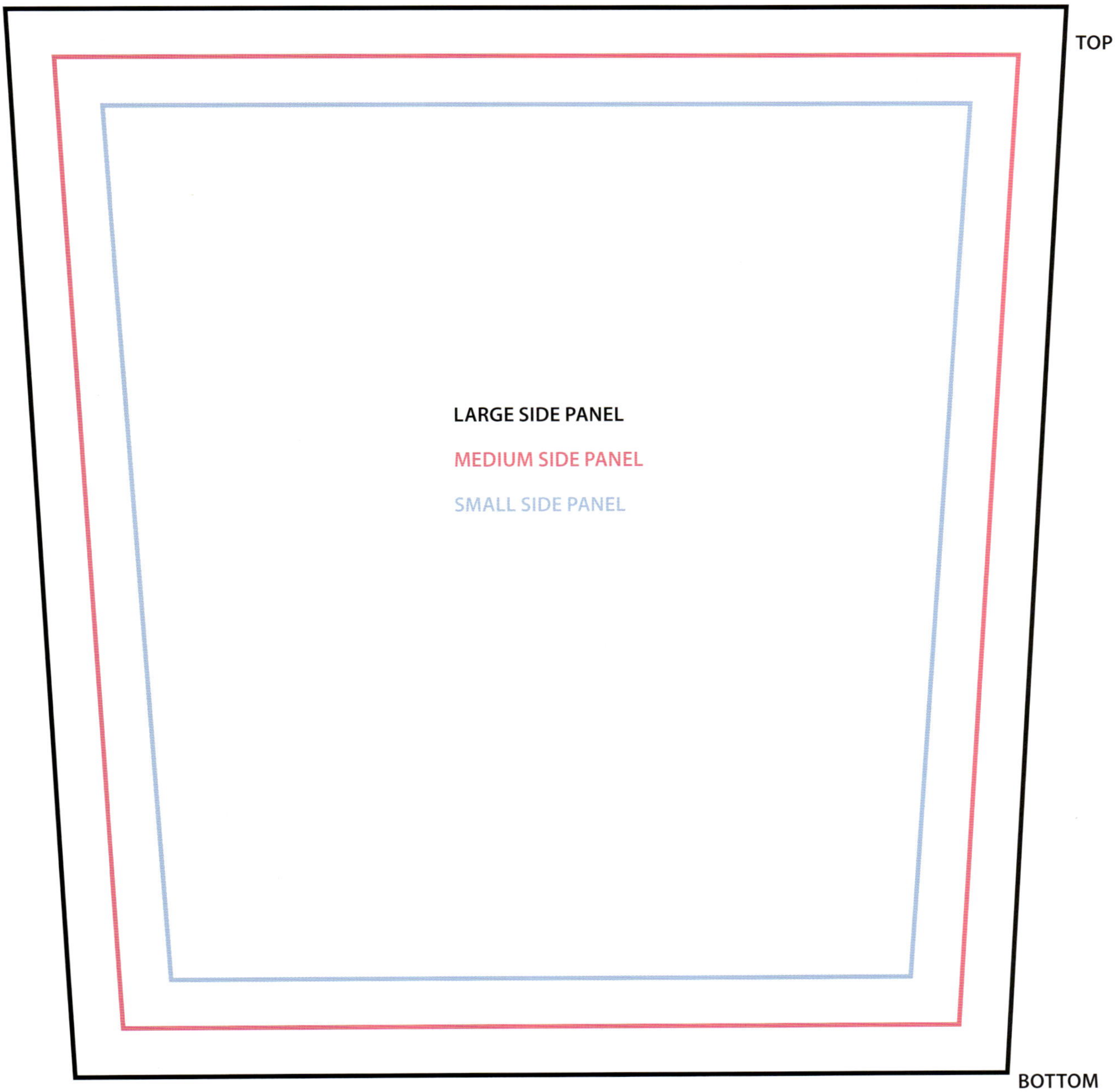

FAUX FUR THROW & PILLOW

Make yourself something truly luxurious this winter. By Jemima Schlee

TIPS

This is a closed pillow–it has no zipper or button fastening–I tend to do this as you get a good even finish on circular pillows. It's not a lot of bother to undo the slipstitching in the seam, remove the pillow insert, clean the cover and replace the insert and stitch the opening closed again.

It's well worth stretching your budget to buy a good quality faux fur – always follow the manufacturer's instructions for cleaning in order to maintain its softness.

YOU WILL NEED

For the pillow:

- 16" x 16" square of faux fur fabric
- 16" x 16" square of satin fabric
- 16" diameter round pillow insert

For the throw:

- $2\frac{3}{8}$ yds of 60" wide faux fur fabric
- $2\frac{1}{4}$ yds of 60" wide satin fabric
- 4 small mother of pearl buttons

For both:

- Sewing thread to match satin fabric
- Sewing machine
- Pins
- Scissors

THE PILLOW

Always match the fabric right sides and raw edges and use a $\frac{1}{2}$" seam allowance when sewing.

1. Cut two 16" diameter circles, one from each fabric. This includes the seam allowances as pillow covers should be slightly smaller than the inserts, ensuring a lovely plump pillow when you finish.
2. Leaving a 4"-5" opening, sew the fabric circles together.
3. Turn the pillow right side out. Tightly roll up your pillow insert and gently ease it through the pillow opening. Once the insert is inside, put your hand into the pillow and arrange the insert so that its contents are evenly distributed within the pillow.
4. Fold the raw edges into the opening and slipstitch the opening closed. Make a row of small Running Stitches around the lining, close to the edge, being careful to pick up the layers of the seam allowances underneath, but not the outer fur.

PHOTOS: EMMA NOREN; STEP PHOTOS: JEMIMA SCHLEE

THE THROW

Always match the fabric right sides and raw edges and use a $\frac{1}{2}$" seam allowance when sewing.

1. Cut the satin lining 54" x 78". Cut the fur 58" x 82". Pin the pieces together along one long edge starting and stopping 2" from each end. Machine stitch the pieces together (*image 1*).

2. Do the same with the opposite long edge.

3. Now prepare the top and bottom seams by pinning the satin 2" from either end with the raw edges aligned. Stitch seam starting and stopping $\frac{1}{2}$" from either end – this will leave a fold of the fur outer fabric at 45° to the corner of your throw (*images 2 & 3*). Leave a 10"-12" gap along one edge for turning right side out.

4. Turn the throw right side out. Using the handle of a wooden spoon, push out the corners of the fur outer fabric, taking care not to push the handle all the way through. Spread your throw out on the floor or a bed fur side down. The fur should fold over to form a "frame" around the satin lining. Fold the raw edges in and slipstitch the opening closed. Make a row of small Running Stitches all around the lining, close to the edge, being careful to pick up the layers of the seam allowances underneath, but not the outer fur (*image 4*).

5. Sew a button into each of the four corners of the lining to anchor them. Stitch all the way through, pushing the hairs of the fur out of the way on the other side so that they don't get caught in your stitches (*image 5*). Take care to not let the the button stitching show on the fur side when you've finished.

PICTURE PERFECT

Make beautiful corsages and keep them in shadow box frames as wall decorations until you want to wear one. By Suzanne Rowland

YOU WILL NEED

- Scraps of fabric, silk, velvet, netting, and lace
- 20" lengths of $1\frac{1}{2}$" wide velvet or grosgrain ribbon
- Felt
- Pin backs
- Vintage buttons and beads
- Feathers
- Craft flower stamens
- Needle and matching thread
- Fabric glue
- Iron

The picture shows the kinds of corsages that can be made; use the instructions to make your own unique pieces, mixing and matching flower styles and adding embellishments like netting, feathers and lace.

1 Cut a $1\frac{3}{4}$"-2" diameter circle of felt. This is the back of the corsage.

2 Sew a pin back just above the center of the felt circle.

3 To make a velvet ribbon rose, place a few spots of glue on the wrong side of the ribbon and twist along the length. Hold one end of the ribbon firmly as you wrap the rest of the ribbon around to form a spiral (*image 1*). Continue wrapping and gluing until you have used the ribbon length. Fold the end under the rose and glue in place.

4 To make a scruffy rose, cut a 2" x 20" bias strip of velvet fabric and fold in half lengthwise. Hold one end firmly and twist the strip loosely. Spiral wrap the strip around the center, forming a rose. Continue twisting, wrapping, and gluing until you have used the ribbon length. Fold the end under the rose and glue in place.

5 To make a neat rose, cut a $2\frac{1}{2}$" x 20" bias strip of velvet fabric. Press the long raw edges to the center. Dot on some glue to keep the edges in place. Repeat the hold, twist, spiral, and gluing process as described in Step 3.

6 To make grosgrain ribbon flowers, use a knotted, doubled thread to sew basting stitches along one long edge of a ribbon length. Pull to gather and join with backstitches (*image 2*).

7 To make small flowers with petals, fold a 3" x 16" fabric strip in half lengthwise. Use a knotted, doubled thread to baste from the folded edge downward, stopping $\frac{1}{4}$" from the raw edges. Baste five continuous triangular shapes along the strip; pull tightly to gather (*image 3*). The space between each triangle forms a flower petal. Join the ends with backstitches.

8 For larger flowers with petals, use a longer, wider fabric strip. Baste the fabric strip in the same technique as Step 7, stitching between the bases of each triangle (*image 4*). Join the ends with backstitches. Flower stamens may be sewn in the center.

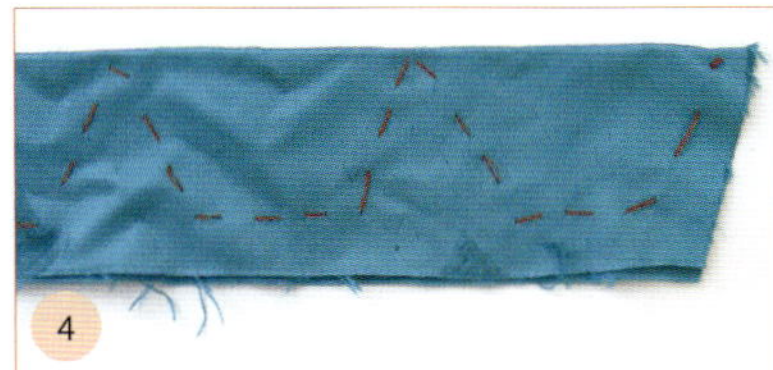

9 To make a leaf, fold a $4\frac{3}{4}$" x $4\frac{3}{4}$" green silk square in half. Then fold into a triangle so that the folded edges meet in the center; pin. Use a knotted, doubled thread to baste along the raw edges (*image 5*). Pull to gather and secure with backstitches.

10 Assemble each corsage by layering leaves, feathers, flowers, and/or netting on the felt circle. Sew each piece in place. Decorate with buttons, pearls, crystals, or beads.

11 Whipstitch around the felt circle to finish (*image 6*).

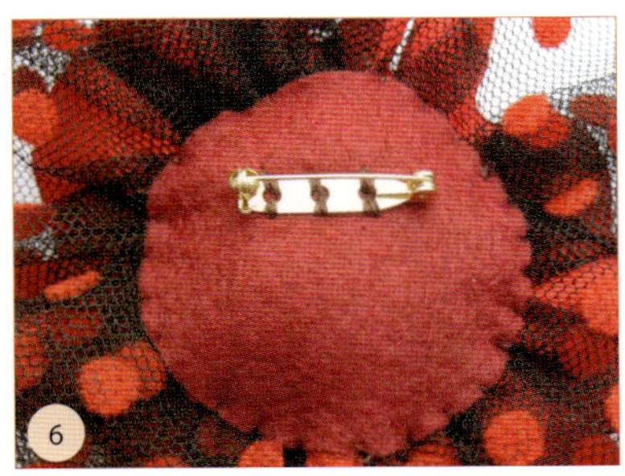

LINEN BUBBLE PILLOWS

Less is more with these chic statement pillows. By Jemima Schlee

YOU WILL NEED

For the square pillow (for the rectangular pillow):

- 55" x 24" (55" x 12") heavy cotton or linen fabric
- 5 7/8" diameter (3 1/2" diameter) buttons from a button cover kit
- 24" x 24" (12" x 24") pillow insert

For the both pillows:

- Sewing thread to match fabric
- Variegated cotton embroidery floss
- White lightweight cotton yarn
- Scissors, pins and a sewing needle
- Sewing machine
- Iron
- Tailor's chalk or air-soluble fabric pen
- Tracing paper

Always match the fabric right sides and raw edges and use a 1/2" seam allowance when sewing.

1 For the square pillow (for the rectangular pillow) cut three pieces from your linen:
Piece A: 24" x 24" (12" x 24")
Piece B: 24" x 11" (12" x 11")
Piece C: 24" x 19" (12" x 19")
This will leave you with a leftover strip of linen for covering your buttons.

2 Zigzag stitch around all raw edges to reduce fraying. Using the chalk, draw a line 3" in from all four edges on the front of fabric piece A to delineate where you will embroider.

3 From tracing paper, cut three circle patterns 2", 3" and 4 1/2" in diameter. With chalk, draw around them randomly on fabric piece A to fill the embroidery area.

4 Thread a needle with the white yarn and tie a knot at one end. Pull the yarn through to the front of the fabric at any point along a drawn circle; remove the needle. Thread the needle with the variegated floss and tie a knot at one end. Bring the needle up through the fabric very close to the start of the white yarn and make small, vertical stitches roughly 1/4" - 3/8" apart along the yarn, securing it to the fabric whilst curving it around to follow the circular chalk line (*image 1*). Continue stitching until the circle is complete, then pull both the floss and the yarn through to the wrong side and tie off.

5 Continue stitching circles of various sizes until your embroidery area is completed.

6 Fold one of the long (short) edges of piece B 1" to the wrong side twice and press. Stitch close to the inside fold.

7 Repeat Step 6 with piece C.

8 Follow the manufacturer's instructions to cover your buttons Stitch a small circle of embroidery around the circumference of each button just as you embroidered circles on piece A (*image 2*).

9 Mark the position and size of each buttonhole along the hemmed edge of piece B. Work buttonholes by hand or machine.

10 Place embroidered piece A right side up. Pin piece B to piece A, aligning the right hand edge. Pin piece C to pieces A and B, aligning the left hand edge.

11 Stitch the pieces together, backstitching over the areas where the three layers overlap for strength. Turn the pillow right side out and press. Sew the buttons to piece C under the buttonholes on piece B. Stuff the pillow with the pillow insert and button the back closure.

1

2

PHOTOS: EMMA NOREN

HAVE A **HOOT**

These handsome fellows will keep your doors propped open and your visitors charmed. Lindy Wells mixes and matches fabrics to create her owl doorstops so that each one develops a character of its own despite being based on the same template. They're a great way of using up leftover fabrics and make a cheerful alternative to a wooden doorstop.

YOU WILL NEED

- Fabric scraps
- Sewing thread
- Two buttons
- 2¼ lbs of uncooked rice
- Polyester fiberfill
- Baby rick rack for wing detail
- Tracing paper
- Sewing machine
- Scissors
- Pinking shears
- Pins
- Thread
- Iron

Always match the fabric right sides and raw edges and use a ¼" wide seam allowance unless indicated otherwise when sewing.

1 Trace the patterns (*page 18*) onto tracing paper; cut out. Or enlarge the patterns as desired. Pin the patterns to your fabrics and cut out the pieces, cutting the eyes and beak with pinking shears.

2 Place each wing on the body as indicated by the blue lines. Machine stitch to the body. Stitch the rick rack along the curved part of each wing.

3 Stitch the eyes to the owl and then sew buttons on the eyes. Place the beak between the eyes and stitch in place.

4 Sew the body and back together along the edges, leaving a 2½" opening at top to turn and stuff.

5 Turn the owl right side out, pour in all the rice and top off with the fiberfill. Slipstitch the opening closed. Now place in front of the door!

PHOTOGRAPHS: PETE JONES

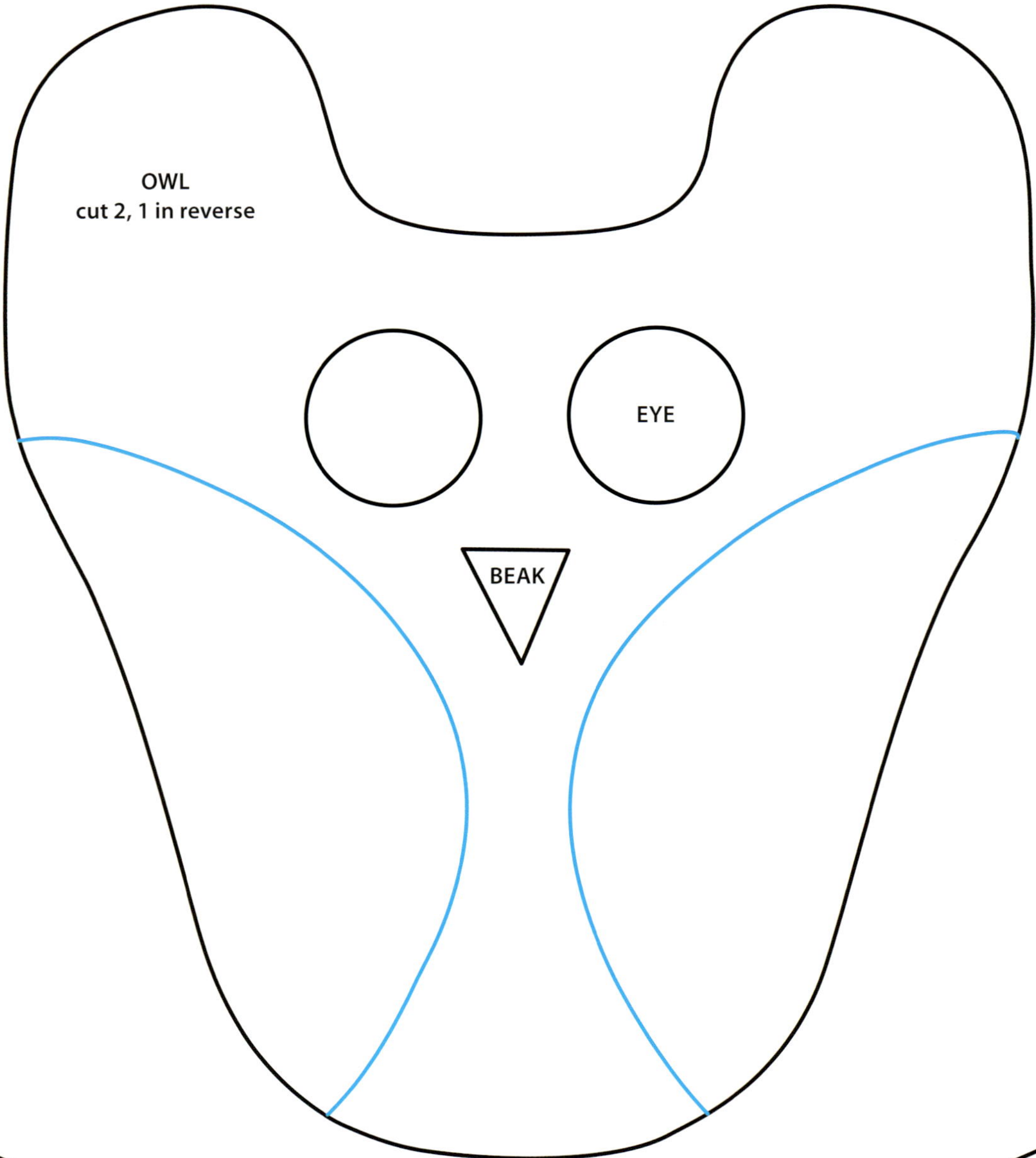

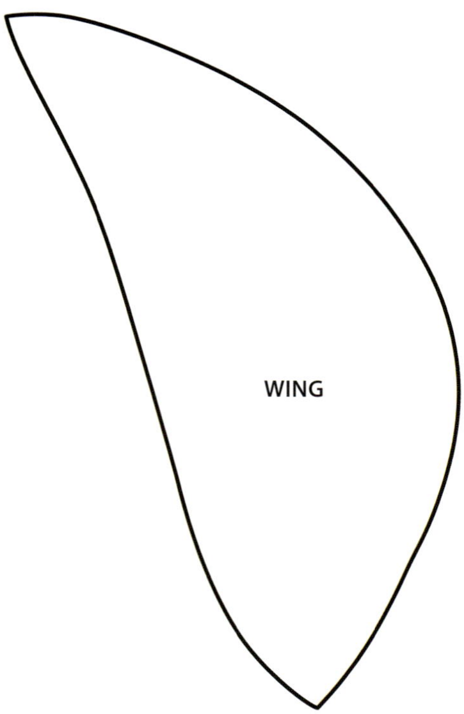

HAVE A HOOT

Enlarge the patterns for the owl on a photocopier to any size you like. You can make little baby owls or a big daddy bird!

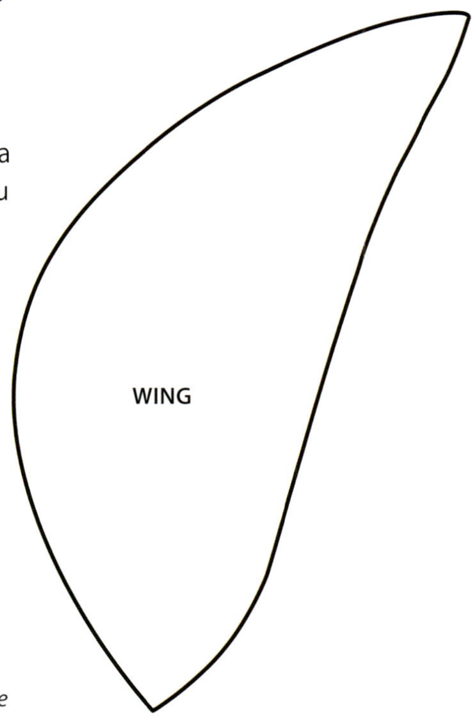

HANGING ORGANIZER

Declutter your bathroom shelves with hanging storage. By Emma Carlow

Clear the decks and decorate your bathroom with this simple sewing project. Made from terry cloth fabric and a regular coat hanger, this soft and washable organizer has a lovely tactile quality and is perfect for keeping all your toiletries organized. Best of all, the organizer is portable; all you need is a hook to hang it on

YOU WILL NEED

- 1 yd of 43"/44"" wide terry cloth fabric
- 4 yds of extra wide double fold bias tape
- Coat hanger
- Thread
- Sewing machine
- Scissors
- Pins
- Iron

Always match the fabric right sides and raw edges and use a 1/2" seam allowance when sewing.

1 Photocopy the pattern pieces (*page 21*) at 250% and cut them out. Lay the pattern pieces on the terry cloth fabric, making sure that the nap of the fabric goes in the same direction on each piece. Pin the patterns down and then cut the pieces out.

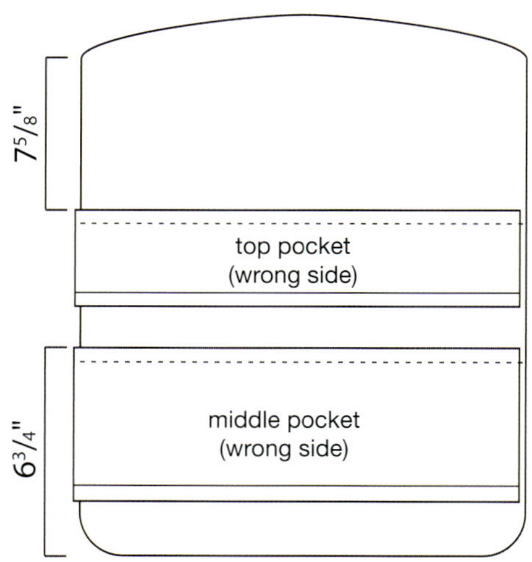

1

2 To attach the bias tape to each pocket top edge, open out the bias tape and pin it with the right side facing the right side of the pocket top. Sew the bias tape to the pocket, stitching in the crease. Fold the bias tape over the raw edges and fold under the raw edge of the bias tape; press. Slipstitch or machine stitch the bias tape in place; press. Repeat for the bottom edge of the back piece.

3 To attach the pockets to the main piece, place the top pocket on the main piece (*image 1*), and stitch along the bottom edge. Fold and press the pocket up. Baste the pocket to the main piece along the side edges. Repeat for the middle pocket. Aligning the side and lower edges, baste the bottom pocket to the main piece.

4 Depending upon what you plan to put in each pocket, mark where you want to stitch the pocket dividers and stitch along the drawn lines.

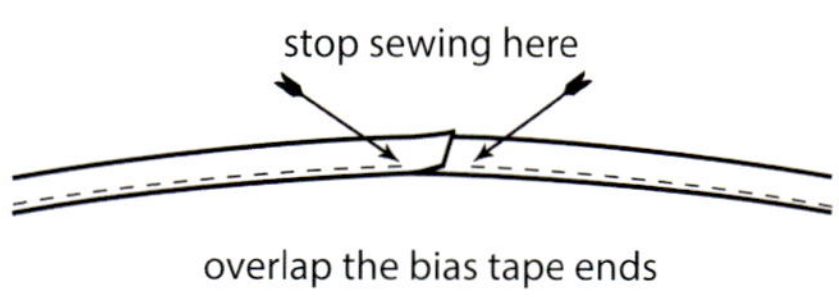

2

5 Aligning the top and side edges, baste the back piece to the wrong side of the main piece. Do not baste along the bottom edge.

6 Attach the bias tape all the way around the organizer as described in step 2, starting at the top center. Leave a small opening at the top center for the coat hanger to slide through. Turn under the raw ends of the bias tape and overlap the ends by about 3/8" (*image 2*). Insert the coat hanger and hand sew the ends of the bias tape together (*image 3*).

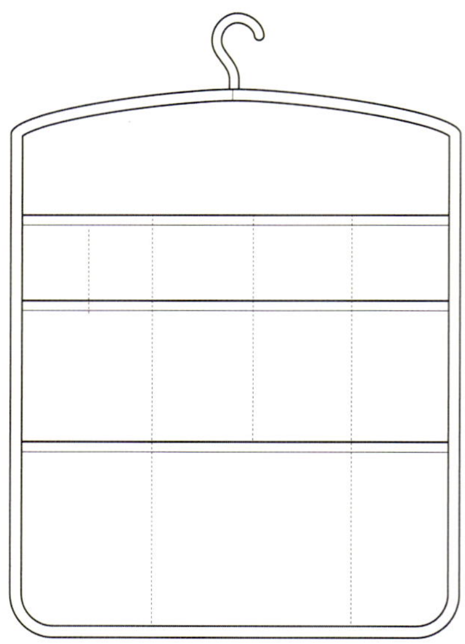

3

HANGING ORGANIZER

Photocopy these patterns at 250%.
You will need to copy the page twice
as the pieces overlap.

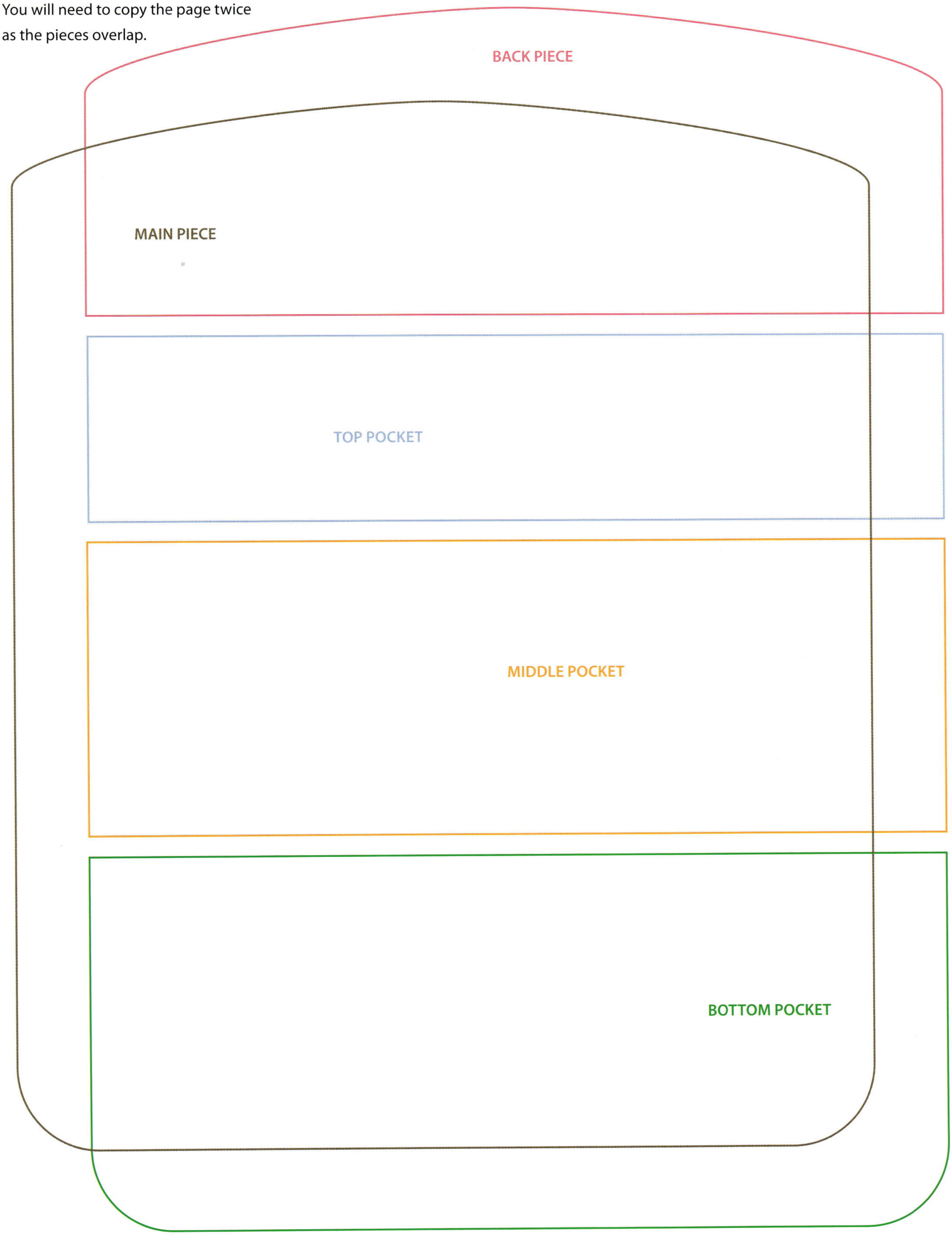

HEADBOARD & DUVET COVER

Make a simple cover that ties at the sides to refresh a tired headboard. By Suzanne Rowland

DUVET COVER

With paper-backed fusible web, you can make appliqués with any fabric and attach them with a hot iron. I chose flower and leaf outlines from the headboard cover fabric to create appliqués for a matching duvet cover.

YOU WILL NEED

- Fabric for appliqués
- Paper-backed fusible web
- Scissors
- Iron
- Pins
- Tracing paper
- Plain duvet cover

1 Draw around the desired shapes from the patterned headboard fabric onto tracing paper and then enlarge on a photocopier or draw freehand if you can. I chose a flower and a leaf outline from the headboard fabric.

2 Once you have the patterns drawn, trace the pieces onto the paper side of the fusible web. Follow the manufacturer's instructions to fuse the web to the wrong side of the appliqué fabrics.

3 Cut out the shapes along the drawn lines. Remove the paper backing from each piece.

4 Lay the duvet cover out on a clean floor and place the appliqué pieces on it. Secure each piece with a couple of pins. Fuse the pieces to the duvet cover.

5 As an extra detail I did a zigzag stitch on the flowers just for decoration.

HEADBOARD COVER

YOU WILL NEED

- Base fabric
- Patterned fabric for center panel
- 5/8" wide ribbon or twill tape
- Matching thread
- Sewing machine
- Scissors
- Pins
- Iron

1 Measure your headboard: measure the width and the height from the mattress to top of the headboard (see the diagram on page 24). The cover will fold over the top of the headboard and down the front and back equally, so if the headboard is a thick one add that in too. Add 1 1/4" to each measurement for the hems. Cut one piece of this size from the base fabric. For the center panel, divide the width measurement into thirds and cut a piece that is the full length (plus 1 1/4" on each end) and one third the width of the base fabric (don't add anything to the width).

2 Press both fabric pieces to remove any creases.

3 Mark the center of each piece by folding it in half widthwise and lightly pressing a crease (*image 1*).

1

4 Working on a flat surface (the floor is ideal) with the right sides facing up, lay the center panel on top of the base fabric and line up the center creases.

5 Smooth out any ripples and pin the center panel in place. Pin down the center as well as around the sides; baste in place if you wish.

6 Sew the center panel in place by topstitching close to the raw edges all the way around.

7 Position the ribbon to cover the raw edges down each side of the panel. Pin in place and machine stitch at either edge (*image 2*).

2

8 For the ties, cut the remaining ribbon into lengths measuring 15" each. I placed three ties on each side; if you have a very deep headboard you may need more. For six ties, you need 12 lengths.

9 Hem one edge of each ribbon length by turning 1/8" to the wrong side twice and machine stitching across the folded edge.

10 Turn the bottom edges of the headboard cover 5/8" to the wrong side twice and press. Machine stitch in place, stitching close to the folded edge.

MAIN PHOTOGRAPH: PETE JONES; STEP PHOTOGRAPHS: BEN ROWLAND

11 For the side edges of the headboard, turn the edges 5/8" to the wrong side twice and press. To mark the position of the ribbon ties, fold the headboard cover in half lengthways. From the fold measure down 4" and mark the position of the first two tapes. Then mark a further two points at 4" intervals towards the hem on either side.

12 Slip the raw edges of each ribbon length under the pressed hem and pin in place (*image 3*).

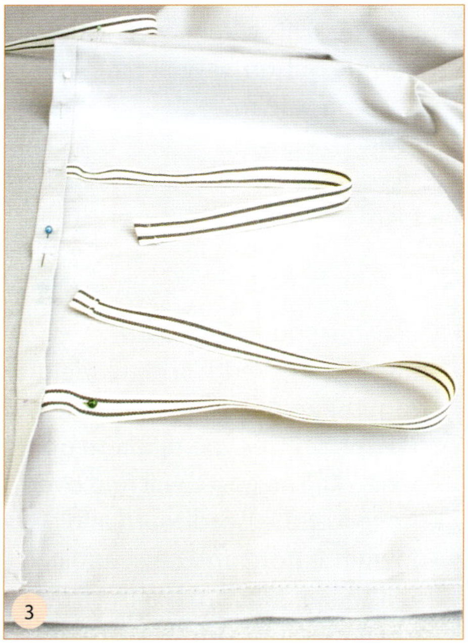

13 Machine stitch along either edge of the hem, catching the ribbons in the stitching. (*image 4*)

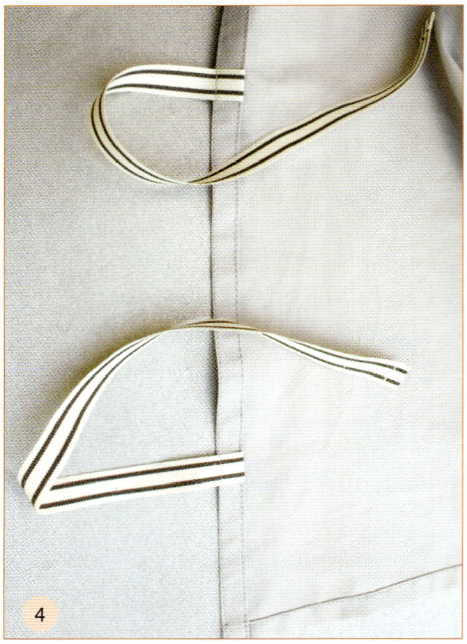

14 Place the cover over your headboard and tie in place.

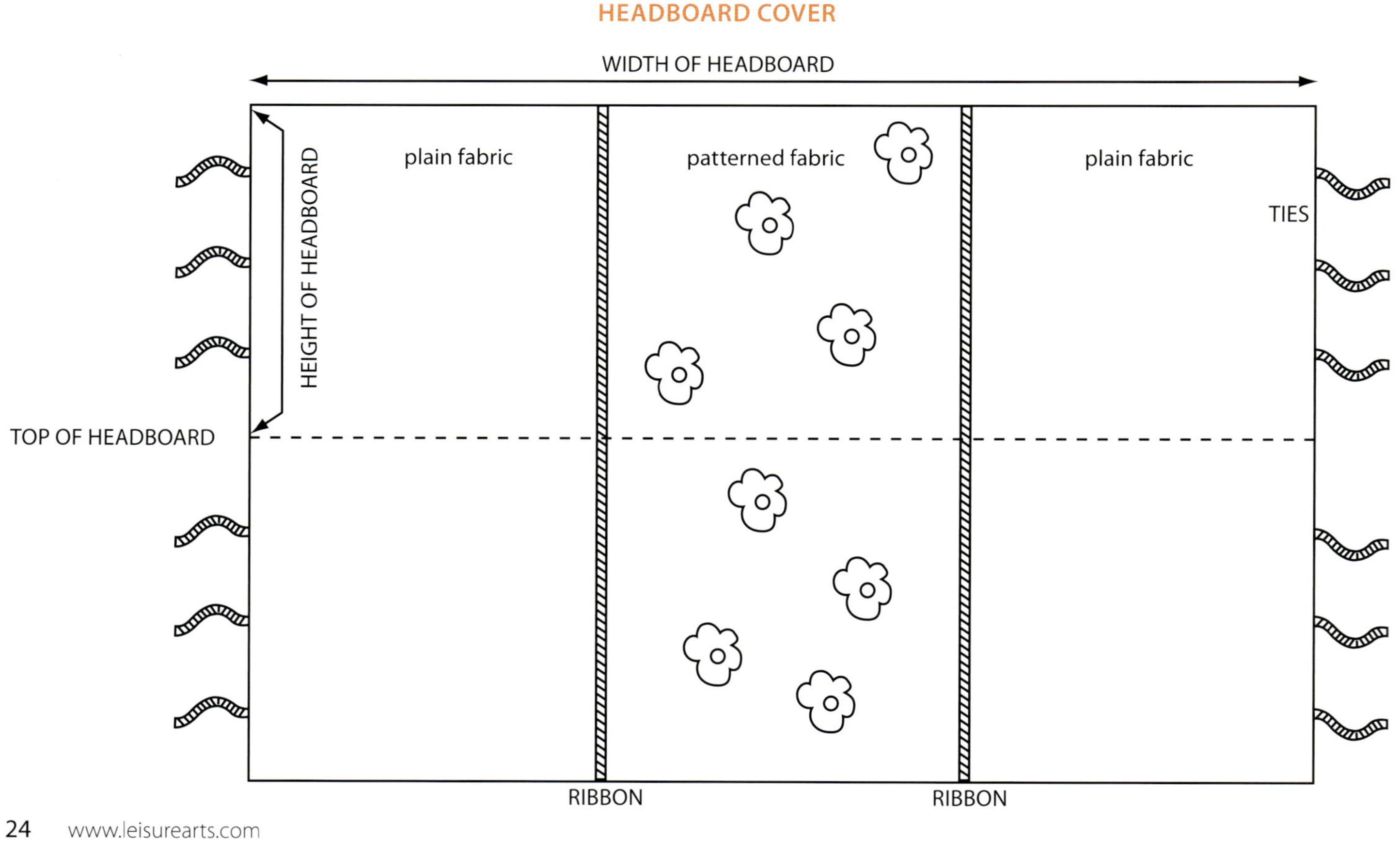

FLOWER POWER PILLOW

Make a rainbow daisy pillow with button centers! By Sian Hamilton

PHOTOGRAPH: LAUREL GUILFOYLE; STEP PHOTOGRAPHS: SIAN HAMILTON

YOU WILL NEED

- 38 1/2" x 17" piece of fabric for pillow cover
- Sewing thread
- Felt scraps
- Buttons
- Scissors
- Needle and pins
- Fusible web tape (optional)
- Tracing paper
- Sewing machine
- Iron

TO MAKE THE FELT FLOWERS

1 The larger flowers are made with five petal pieces and the smaller ones from one circular piece (*image 1*).

2 To make a small flower, draw around anything you like that is approximately 3 1/2" diameter, straight onto the felt using a black felt tip pen. I used the outside of a large roll of tape (*image 2*).

3 Cut out the circle and either divide the shape into five sections with a protractor or by eye marking the edge of the felt circle. I went by eye, cutting slits where I thought they should be; I like the fact that all the petals are not perfectly the same. Leave a center area about 3/4" diameter uncut. When the five sections are cut, round the edges off again by eye (*image 3*).

4 Thread a needle with a contrasting color thread and fold a petal in half. Starting about 3/8" from the flower center, work 5 deep Blanket Stitches (*see box, page 27*). Repeat for each petal (*image 4*). Turn the flower over so the stitching is on the wrong side and sew the button in the center of the flower. Make up as many as you like, vary the size of the flowers for effect.

5 To make a large flower, trace the petal pattern (*page 27*) and cut out. Draw around the pattern 5 times on the felt. Cut the petals out. Using the same technique as for a small flower, fold each petal in half and work about 5 Blanket Stitches starting about 3/8" from the pointed end (*image 5*). Stitch all 5 petals in this manner.

6 Place two petals together with the blanket stitched edges facing up. Work Blanket Stitches from the point toward the opposite edge for about 3/8" (*image 6*). Open up the petals and add another one using the same technique. Continue to add petals and you'll see the flower is forming. Once you have added the fifth petal, join the first petal to the fifth to complete the flower. Sew a button in the center.

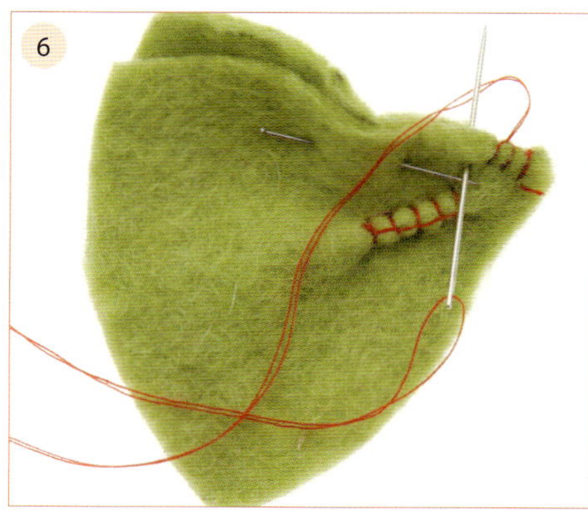

7 Lay your pillow cover on a table and place the flowers in a pleasing arrangement. Take them off one by one and lay down in the same pattern on the table. This will allow you to follow your design as you attach the flowers to the pillow cover.

8 Sew each flower to the pillow cover by sewing from inside of the cover: come up through the pillow cover, through the flower back and under the button. Don't try to stitch through the button, but bring the needle up behind the button. I made about 5 stitches each time coming up underneath the button at a different point. Secure and clip the thread.

TO MAKE A PILLOW COVER

Always match the fabric right sides and raw edges and use a $\frac{1}{2}$" wide seam allowance when sewing.

1 Cut a piece of fabric $38\frac{1}{2}$" x 17". Press both short ends $1\frac{1}{4}$" to the wrong side. Then either topstitch the hems or use fusible web tape to fuse the hems in place as I did.

2 Matching the right sides, fold one end over 12" and the other end over 8". Sew the side seams. Turn the pillow cover right side out and press.

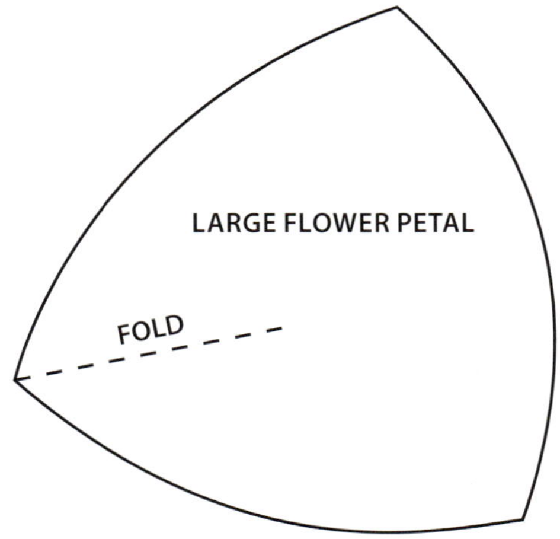

BLANKET STITCH TECHNIQUE

To do a blanket stitch, thread needle and knot the thread end. Push the needle through the fabric close to the edge and take a tiny stitch to secure the thread. Push the needle back straight through the fabric and before you pull it right through bring the thread behind the needle. As you then pull the thread tight it will be caught behind itself. If right handed, work from right to left; work vice versa for left-handers.

FRENCH-STYLE LINEN TOWEL

Make your own vintage French-style linen hand towel scattered with simple embroidered spring flowers. By Jemima Schlee

YOU WILL NEED

- 51" x $10\frac{3}{4}$" piece of grey linen
- Grey and white sewing thread
- Sewing machine
- Quilting guide (see tip)
- Sharp scissors
- Embroidery and sewing needles
- White embroidery floss
- Towel holder with removable bar

1 Join the two short edges of your linen with a flat-fell seam. With *wrong* sides together and using a $\frac{1}{2}$" seam allowance, sew the short edges together with grey thread. Trim one seam allowance to a scant $\frac{1}{4}$" (*image 1*).

1

2 Press $\frac{1}{4}$" to the wrong side on the larger seam allowance. Fold and press the larger seam allowance to the right side, concealing the smaller seam allowance. Stitch along the folded edge (*image 2*).

2

3 Press the two long raw edges $\frac{3}{8}$" to the wrong side twice. Topstitch these hems.

4 To stitch the white checked design on your towel, use white thread to stitch small close zigzag stitch vertical lines $1\frac{1}{4}$" from one long edge, and then at $2\frac{1}{4}$" intervals– the last line should be $1\frac{1}{4}$" from the opposite long edge.

5 Straight stitch horizontal lines $2\frac{1}{4}$" apart in the same manner.

6 Now add more vertical lines across this grid in white thread using straight stitches – start $2\frac{1}{4}$" from the long edge. Add lines in straight stitching centered between the horizontal lines.

7 Finish the towel by stitching a scallop stitch close to each long edge (*image 3*).

3

8 Embroider scattered flowers (refer to the diagram, right) randomly within the sewn grid and rotating the flowers to add variation.

TIP

I have a nifty attachment on my sewing machine used for quilting, which helps you stitch at a fixed measurement – perfect for parallel lines of stitches. It's well worth investing in one of these if you do a lot of quilting.

FLOWERS TO EMBROIDER

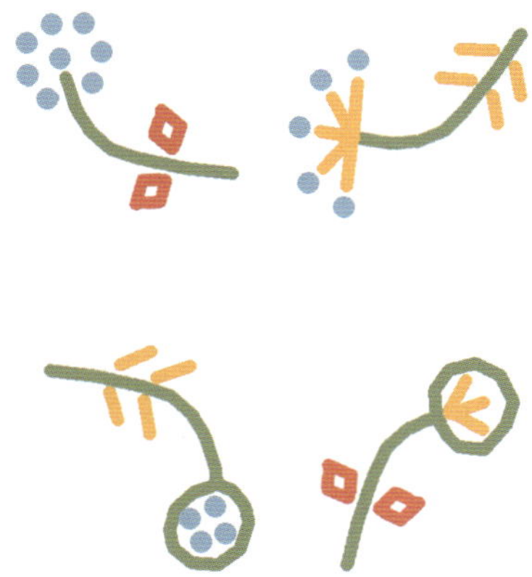

= Couching Stitch

= Straight Stitch

= Lazy Daisy Stitch

= French Knot

STEP-BY-STEP PHOTOGRAPHS: JEMIMA SCHLEE

HERB BAG

A simple rustic folk-style bag is the perfect place to store freshly cut herbs.
By Jemima Schlee

YOU WILL NEED

- 9" x 12" piece of natural-colored linen
- 9" x 12" piece of ecru-colored linen for lining
- 6" length of 2" wide trim
- 12" length of jute twine
- Red embroidery floss
- Sewing machine
- Scissors
- Iron
- Sewing needle, thread and pins
- Tracing paper

PATTERN CUTTING

Photocopy the pattern (page 32) at 166% and cut out. Use the pattern to cut the following:

Pattern piece A (black outline) – cut two in natural linen (outer fabric); cut 1 in ecru linen (lining fabric)

Pattern piece B (black outline with pink teardrop opening) – cut 1 in ecru linen (lining fabric)

Always match the fabric right sides and raw edges and use a 1/4" seam allowance when sewing unless indicated otherwise.

TO MAKE

1 Lay lining piece B on top of one outer piece A placing the right sides together. Align the outside edges and pin together (*image 1*).

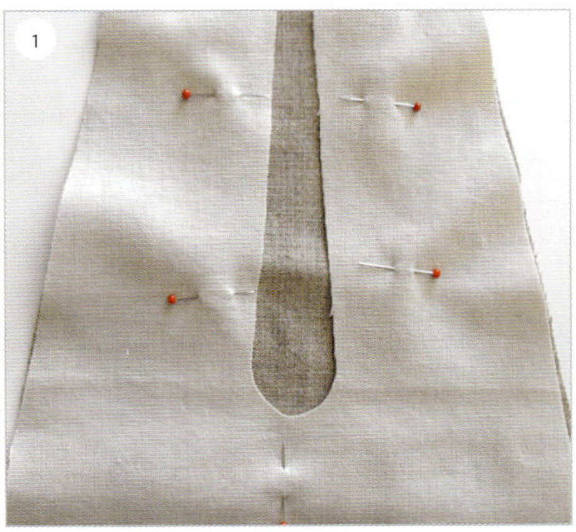

2 Stitch a seam 1/4" in from the teardrop opening edge of the lining piece B. Trim the outer piece A even with the edge of the lining piece B and make small snips in the seam allowances just to the stitching line around the curved edge – take great care not to actually cut the stitches (*image 2*).

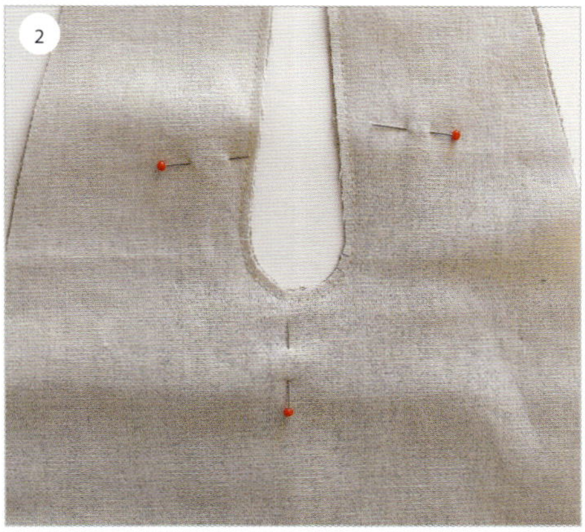

3 Matching the right sides, place the remaining outer piece A on the outer piece. Pin the outside edges of both pieces together – at the same time being careful that the lining piece B is not caught in the pins (*image 3*). Stitch this seam, being careful that the lining is not caught in the seam.

4 Matching right sides, place the lining piece A on lining piece B. Pin the outside edges of both pieces together (*image 4*). Stitch this seam.

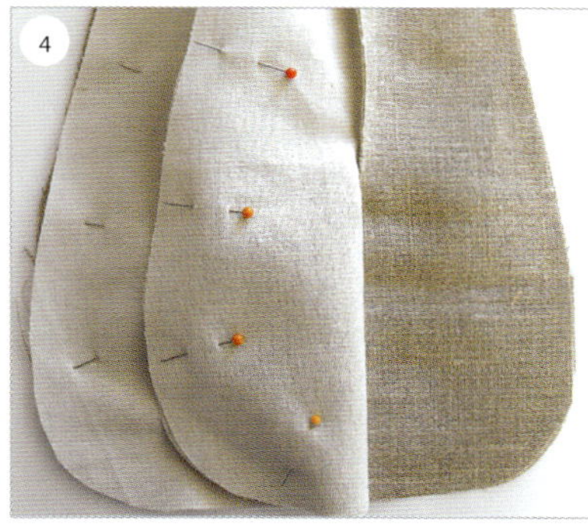

5 Cut small "V" shapes out of the seam allowances of the bottom curves of the outer fabric only (*image 5*).

6 Press the outer seam allowances of both the outer fabric and lining open. Turn the bag right side out through the opening at the top and push the lining to the inside. Use a chop stick or knitting needle to push out the curves and to shape the edges. Give the bag a good press and baste around the teardrop edge and along the top edge (*image 6*).

MAIN PHOTOS: EMMA NOREN; STEP-BY-STEP PHOTOS: JEMIMA SCHLEE

7 Cut the trim 1" longer than the top edge of the bag. Matching the long edges, fold the trim in half and place it over the bag raw edges. Open the trim out, still in position, and pin it along the front edge with the two raw ends folded under. Machine stitch from the top of the trim, down one folded end, across the top of the bag and back up the other folded edge (*image 7*).

8 Turn the bag over and fold the trim down to encase the top edges of the bag. Thread the jute length through the trim channel. Securely hand sew the trim edges to the bag (*image 8*).

9 Decorate the teardrop opening by working Running Stitches and Lazy Daisy stitches to create small blossoms, using 6 strands of embroidery floss.

Guild of Master Craftsman Publications Ltd. and Leisure Arts, Inc., grants permission to the owner of this book to photocopy the patterns on page 32 for personal use only.

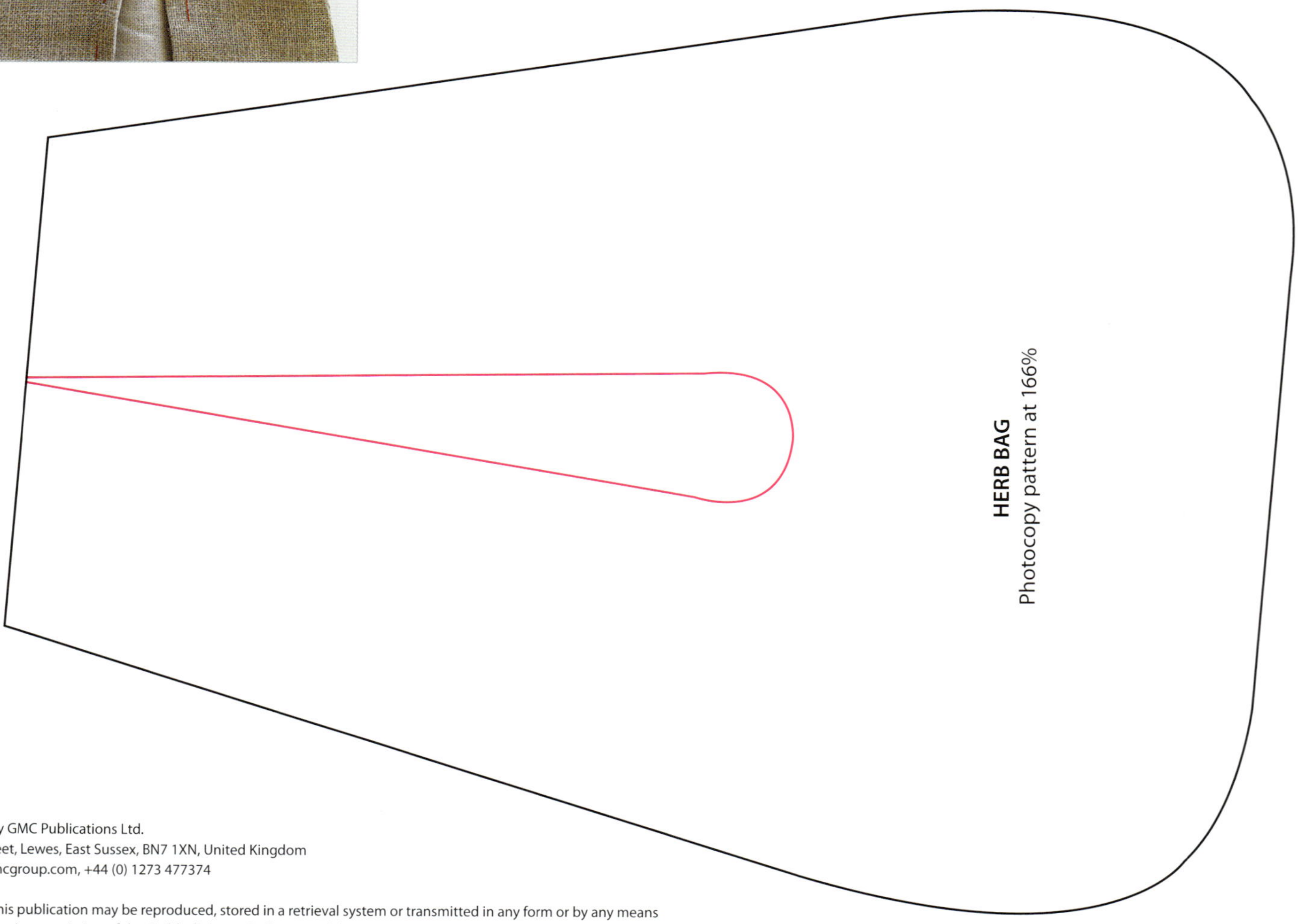

Produced by GMC Publications Ltd.
86 High Street, Lewes, East Sussex, BN7 1XN, United Kingdom
www.thegmcgroup.com, +44 (0) 1273 477374